MW01537817

Study Guide for
Wuthering Heights

— *by Charlotte Brontë* —

Edited by
Patience DeMasi
Joseph Pearce

Introduction by
Patrick S. J. Carmack

IGNATIUS PRESS   SAN FRANCISCO

Cover design by John Herreid

ISBN 978-1-58617-310-4

Printed in the United States of America ∞

Table of Contents

Why a Great Books Study Guide?

Wisdom is generally acknowledged to be the highest good of the human mind, whether this be recognized as knowledge of first principles and causes or as a contemplative gaze at Wisdom itself. But how does one obtain wisdom? The means is primarily conversation with great and wise persons who have already advanced far along the paths of knowledge and understanding to wisdom. As the philosopher Dr. Peter Redpath succinctly puts it when addressing audiences of young people interested in understanding why they ought to read great books, "If you wish to become wise, learn from wise people."

Since, however, persons of great wisdom are rare and generally unavailable to us due to distance or death, we enter into conversation with them through their books which record their thought. In doing this, we soon discover how all the authors of great books used this same method of study themselves. They began by conversing with or reading the great books written by the sages of earlier generations. In so doing, they avoided having to re-invent the wheel each generation; and they avoided making mistakes already dealt with and were able to build on existing foundations. Indeed what would be the point in studying mediocre works by lesser luminaries or beginning all thought over from square one every few years, when great books by the wisest people—the great sages of civilization—are readily available?

> The reading of all good books is indeed like a conversation with the noblest men of past centuries who were the authors of them, nay a carefully studied conversation, in which they reveal to us none but the best of their thoughts. (Rene Descartes, *Discourse on Method*)

Through the internal dialectical process found in the great books—
the references, discussions, critiques, and responses to the thought
of the authors' wise predecessors, a process referred to as the "Great
Conversation" by Robert M. Hutchins—we may closely follow
the development of the investigations conducted by these wise
men into the great ideas they have pondered and about which they
have written. This manner of study has always been the normative
approach to wisdom in the West.

> Until lately the West has regarded it as self-evident that the road
> to education lay through great books. No man was educated until
> he was acquainted with the masterpieces of his tradition. . . . They
> were the principal instruments of liberal education. . . . The goal
> toward which Western society moves is the Civilization of the
> Dialogue. The spirit of Western civilization is the spirit of inquiry.
> Its dominant element is *Logos*.[1]

No ongoing dialogue comparable in duration or breadth exists in
the East. Pope Benedict XVI has mentioned that Western civilization has become the dominant civilization because of its closer
correspondence to human nature. In his 2006 Regensburg lecture,
he noted that there exists a real analogy between our created reason
and God, who is *Logos* (meaning both "reason" and "word"). To
abandon reason—and hence the dialogue, which is both reason's
natural expression and necessary aid—would be contrary both to
the nature of man and of God. This cumulative wisdom of the
West is preserved and transmitted in its great music and art, but
most particularly in the study of its great books which record the
results of three millennia of dialogue, guided by reason, concern-
ing the most profound ideas with which we must all grapple such
as existence, life, love, happiness, and so forth.

---

[1] Robert M. Hutchins, *The Great Conversation: The Substance of a Liberal Education,*
vol. 1, *The Great Books of the Western World* (Chicago: Encyclopedia Brittannica, Inc.,
1952).

This manner of learning is greatly facilitated when the reader also engages in a dialectic exchange—a live conversation (in person or now online)—with other readers of the same books, probing and discussing the great ideas contained in them and, one hopes, carrying them a few steps further. This method of learning is often referred to as the Socratic method, after the ancient Athenian philosopher Socrates, who initiated its use as a deliberate way to obtain understanding and wisdom through mutual inquiry and discussion. This same "questioning" method was used by Christ, who often answered questions with other questions, parables, and stories that left the hearers wondering, questioning, and thinking. He already knew the answers, as Socrates often did. The goal was not merely indoctrination of the memory with information, facts, and knowledge, but mind- and life-changing understanding and wisdom.

This study guide is intended for students (if one is still learning, one is a student) who have read—extensively—lesser works, particularly the classic children's literature. Given that degree of preparation, students of high school age and older, including adults, can pick up Homer's *Iliad* and *Odyssey* or Herodotus' *Histories* and other great works and enter into the seminal thought of the most influential books of our culture and civilization. There is reason not to delay such education.

The great books are, for the most part, the most interesting and well written of all books. They were not written for experts. Their wide and enduring appeal to generation after generation testifies to that fact. Readers reasonably prepared for them will find them captivating, entertaining, and enlightening. Naturally, some readers will profit more than others from the great books, but all will profit from learning about the Trojan War, ancient civilizations, the heroes of ancient Greece, the early tragedies, and the thought of Aristotle. Works such as Genesis, the *Aeneid*, Saint Augustine's *Confessions*, Chaucer's *Canterbury Tales*, Dante's *Divine Comedy*, Saint Thomas Aquinas' *Summa theologica*, and Shakespeare's plays are foundational for and/or profoundly influential on our way of life. These works are essential for participation in the Great Conversation mentioned above. The enduring intellectual dialogue begins with the works of Homer, the "father of civilization", and proceeds through the centuries, eventually absorbing the Old and New Testaments in a lengthy reformulation of classical civilization into Western civilization, which continues—albeit always under assault by various errors—right up to our time.

The principal guides in selecting the works of enduring appeal to be included in the corpus of great books, besides generations of readers, include the late, great Dr. Mortimer J. Adler, who worked for eighty years (from 1921 to 2000, when I had the privilege to participate in his last Socratic discussion groups) to restore and keep the great classics, including particularly those by Plato, Aristotle, and Aquinas, in the Western canon of great books. As Dr. Adler put it, "The great books constitute the backbone of a liberal education." But read alone in our postmodernist context of radical skepticism, the great books can easily be misunderstood and used for all manner of mischief. It was precisely a desire to provide a deeper understanding of the importance and influence of the great books—to highlight what is true and great in them and to expose and defang what is false—that inspired Ignatius Press to initiate its important Critical Editions series.

Augmenting the work of Dr. Adler, on behalf of Ignatius Press, is Joseph Pearce, the author of several critically acclaimed, best-selling biographies of great authors, who has diligently worked as the author and/or editor of these study guides to accompany the Ignatius Critical Editions, of which he is also the series editor. Our gratitude extends to Father Joseph Fessio for his encouragement of this much-needed project, which is so broad in scope and vision as to be potentially revolutionary in the schools, colleges, and universities dominated by relativism. Homeschoolers, though somewhat shielded from the relativism of the schools, will find in these guides a welcome and trustworthy means of introduction to the great books and to their careful and critical reading.

Finally, it is worth emphasizing that these Ignatius Critical Editions Study Guides are merely introductory guides with tests, questions, and answer keys helpful for student assessment. The great books themselves are the primary texts, their authors our primary teachers.

Patrick S. J. Carmack
January 18, 2008

Patrick S. J. Carmack, J.D., is the president of the Great Books Academy Homeschool Program (greatbooksacademy.org), the Angelicum Academy Homeschool Program (angelicum.net), the Western Civilization Foundation, and the online publication *Classical Homeschooling Magazine* (classicalhomeschooling.com).

How to Use This Guide

The Ignatius Critical Editions (ICE) Study Guides are intended to assist students and teachers in their reading of the Ignatius Critical Editions. Each guide gives a short introductory appraisal of the contextual factors surrounding the writing of the literary work, a short "bare bones" summary of the plot, and a more in-depth summary of some of the essential critical aspects of the work. There is also a list of things to think about while reading the book, designed to focus the reader's critical faculties. These points to ponder will enable the reader to rise above a merely recreational reading of the text to a level of critical and literary appreciation befitting the work itself.

Finally, there are questions for the student to answer. These fall into two distinct categories: questions concerned with a knowledge of the *facts* of the work, and questions concerned with analyzing the *truths* that emerge from the work. This approach is rooted in the fundamental axiom, taught by great philosophers such as Aristotle and Saint Thomas Aquinas, that we must go *through* the facts *to* the truth. Put simply, an inadequate knowledge of the facts of a work (who did what and when, who said what to whom, etc.) will inevitably lead to a failure to understand the work on its deeper levels of meaning.

As such, readers of the work are strongly encouraged to answer all the *fact-related* questions in part 1. The close reading of the text that this will entail will prepare them for the essay questions in part 2. With regard to the latter, it is left to the discretion of the teacher (or the reader) as to how many of these questions should be answered. Some of the questions, particularly those calling for a contextual reading of the work in relation to other works, might be unsuitable for less-advanced students or readers. In such cases, the teacher (or reader) should use his discretion in deciding which of the essay questions should be answered. In any event, you have been provided with an abundance of questions from which to choose!

Teachers should also be aware that the answer key can be removed before the study guide is made available to the student. Answers to the questions in the "Bare Bones" and "Things to Think About" sections are not included in the answer key because these questions are intended to raise issues for the student to ponder and are not intended to be employed for examination purposes.

It should be noted that the Ignatius Critical Editions and the ICE Study Guides approach these great works of literature from a tradition-oriented perspective. Those seeking deconstruction, "queer theory", feminism, postcolonialism, and other manifestations of the latest academic fads and fashions will be disappointed. If you are unable to think outside the postmodern box, this guide is not for you!

Context

The fifth child of Patrick and Maria Brontë, Emily was born in Yorkshire, England, in 1818. Her family lived in Haworth, Yorkshire, where her father had received a permanent position as pastor. Emily's mother died when she was three. Emily and all but one of her sisters were sent to boarding school, from which the two eldest returned ill and died soon after. Emily and Charlotte returned home to finish their education. Later, Charlotte and Emily went to the Continent, to Brussels, to study languages. After their return, Emily remained at her home until her death in 1848 of tuberculosis, a year after the publication of *Wuthering Heights*.

Described by her sister as one who was never truly happy or at rest when away from her home, Emily led a largely solitary life, leaving fairly little behind by way of understanding either her or her writing. Her life, although simple, was heavily marked with suffering. Having lost her mother, two of her sisters, and her brother, Emily was well acquainted with the unyielding trials of life. Yet her passage through these trials served not to weaken her faith and vision of goodness but to strengthen it. It was not a strengthening, however, that achieved its end by turning away from the darkness and harshness of life. Its victory, rather, was attained through an unflinching acknowledgment of the reality of sin and the darkness it brings and, in spite of it, seeing the ultimate goodness that triumphs eternally over all. *Wuthering Heights* is dark—much of Emily Brontë's poetry is dark as well—yet it is truth and goodness that are left standing in the end, as the vanity and meanness of the world pass away.

Emily Brontë's novel *Wuthering Heights* reflects a profound understanding of the human person and the drama of sin and redemption. Its context is the context of her own life, passed largely "in the absolute retirement of a village parsonage, amongst the hills".[1] Emily had ample experience of human nature and its condition to fashion her well-wrought plot and its conclusion. The fruit of an avid imagination and profound understanding of sin and suffering, *Wuthering Heights* is indeed a dark and often disturbing tale, yet ultimately it is faith and love that give this novel its true significance and meaning. For though Emily Brontë in *Wuthering Heights* starkly portrays the effects of the brutal cycles of sin and bondage, her vision within the novel penetrates to a deeper reality as sin is undone by love and its bonds are broken through forgiveness.

---

[1] Emily Brontë, *Wuthering Heights*, ed. Ian Jack, with an introduction and notes by Patsy Stoneman, Oxford World's Classics (New York: Oxford University Press, 1998), p. 371.

Bare Bones: The Skeleton Plot

Wuthering Heights is an intricately woven tale of two families, the Earnshaws and the Lintons.

The story opens with Mr. Lockwood, tenant of Thrushcross Grange, paying a visit to Mr. Heathcliff, his landlord and the master of Wuthering Heights. Mr. Lockwood introduces the story and the major characters of it. He is, like the reader, utterly ignorant of the family residing at Wuthering Heights and of the family's history. He quickly discovers Wuthering Heights is a place of darkness and mystery, haunted and restless. Determined to know more, Mr. Lockwood appeals to Nelly Dean, who served both families, to shed light on their past. At this point, the narration is taken over by Nelly Dean, who begins her tale with the arrival of Heathcliff at Wuthering Heights.

Heathcliff is brought as a child to Wuthering Heights by Mr. Earnshaw, who "took to Heathcliff strangely" (see *Wuthering Heights*, p. 46). From the beginning, the presence of Heathcliff causes division and strife within the family, particularly between Mr. Earnshaw's own children, Hindley and Catherine. There is nothing but antagonism between Heathcliff and Hindley. Catherine, though despising Heathcliff at first, quickly becomes inseparable from him, defending him, though also using her influence over him to tease and distress her father.

After the death of Mr. Earnshaw, Hindley reduces Heathcliff to the status of a servant, degrading him to such an extent that "he acquired a slouching gait, and ignoble look; his naturally reserved disposition was exaggerated into an almost idiotic excess" (see *Wuthering Heights*, p. 79). Catherine at this time develops a friendship with the Linton children, Isabella and Edgar. Though she and Heathcliff remain close, Catherine begins to lead a double life, wild and unruly with Heathcliff but gentle and well-mannered with the Lintons.

As Edgar and Catherine become closer, he proposes to her. Catherine agrees to marry Edgar, knowing she is wrong in doing so. She loves Heathcliff, and had he not been so degraded, she would not have thought of marrying anyone else. She confesses her love to Nelly Dean: "I've no more business to marry Edgar Linton than I have to be in heaven. . . . [I]t would degrade me to marry Heathcliff, now; so he shall never know how I love him . . . because he's more myself than I am" (see *Wuthering Heights*, p. 92). Heathcliff leaves Wuthering Heights after overhearing Catherine's confession that it would "degrade" her to marry him.

Catherine falls seriously ill when she discovers Heathcliff is gone. After her recovery, she marries Edgar and goes to live at Thrushcross Grange. They live peacefully enough until Heathcliff's return three years later.

Heathcliff has acquired considerable wealth during his absence. He takes up residence at Wuthering Heights with Hindley, who tolerates his old enemy because Heathcliff's wealth enables Hindley to indulge his drinking and gambling habits. Heathcliff visits Catherine frequently, to the great discomfort of both Edgar and Nelly Dean, who foresees no good coming of Heathcliff's return. Though he appears refined and has "retained no marks of former degradation", there is yet a "half-civilized ferocity" that lingers in his countenance (see *Wuthering Heights*, p. 110).

Nelly Dean describes Heathcliff's return to Wuthering Heights as "an oppression past explaining. I felt that God had forsaken the stray sheep there to its own wicked wanderings, and an evil beast prowled between it and the fold, waiting his time to spring and destroy" (see *Wuthering Heights*, p. 122). She recognizes in Heathcliff the same vindictiveness that marked his childhood.

Heathcliff has returned to wreak his vengeance on the Earn-shaw and Linton families. He enacts his plans differently, however, than he had originally intended, after Catherine's warm greet-ing. He tells Catherine that he came "to settle . . . with Hind-ley; and then prevent the law by doing execution on myself. Your welcome has put these ideas out of my mind" (see *Wuthering Heights*, p. 111). Working, then, in a more subtle way, Heathcliff begins by encouraging Hindley's drinking and gambling, loaning him money and eventually holding the mortgage on Wuthering Heights. He attaches Hindley's son, Hareton, to himself, to carry out his revenge on Hindley through the degradation of his son. Yet he builds his plans quietly and bides his time, doing nothing drastic for Catherine's sake.

Eventually Heathcliff's visits at Thrushcross Grange become unbearable to Edgar, particularly after Heathcliff encourages Isabella, Edgar's sister, who fancies herself in love with Heathcliff. Heathcliff is subsequently denied access to Thrushcross Grange, and after a violent scene in which Edgar strikes him, Heathcliff leaves.

Catherine becomes dangerously ill with brain fever after the scene between Heathcliff and her husband. Her illness breaks her, and she never quite recovers. Though he is warned that Catherine will never fully recover, that he will be saving only "a mere ruin of humanity", Edgar perseveres devotedly in nursing her back to health, knowing "no limits in gratitude and joy" (see *Wuthering Heights*, p. 150) when Catherine's life is finally out of danger.

Meanwhile, Isabella elopes with Heathcliff. They settle at Wuthering Heights, where Isabella is quite miserable as she comes to understand the heartless cruelty of the person she has married. Meanwhile, Heathcliff contrives a way to see Catherine, inducing Nelly to warn him of when Edgar will be away.

Catherine's illness has changed her drastically. Heathcliff real-izes upon his entrance that "there was no prospect of ultimate recovery there—she was fated, sure to die" (see *Wuthering Heights*, p. 177). This meeting between Heathcliff and Catherine epitomizes in many ways the whole of their relationship. They torment each other together, yet they cannot bear separation. Catherine tells Heathcliff: "I wish I could hold you . . . till we were both dead! I shouldn't care what you suffered. I care nothing for your suffering" (see *Wuthering Heights*, p. 178). Heathcliff responds, while "covering her with frantic caresses", "You teach me now how cruel you've been—cruel and false. . . . I have not one word of comfort—you deserve this" (see *Wuthering Heights*, p. 180). Heathcliff is forced to leave, however, by the arrival of Edgar. Catherine has fainted, and Heathcliff deposits her "lifeless-looking form" (see *Wuthering Heights*, p. 182) in Edgar's arms as Edgar enters, Healthcliff departing to keep vigil in the garden.

Catherine dies that same night and gives birth prematurely to a girl. Edgar names the child Catherine ("Cathy"), after her mother. He grieves the death of his wife, yet it does not destroy him. He takes joy in the child left behind. He becomes resigned with time, recalling his wife's memory with tenderness and love. Heathcliff, however, is tortured. His prayer is that Catherine may "wake in torment" (see *Wuthering Heights*, p. 187), and he begs her ghost to haunt him, Heathcliff saying he is unable to live without his "life", without his "soul".

Isabella flees Wuthering Heights and Heathcliff after Catherine's death. Moving far out of Heathcliff's reach, she gives birth to a son, whom she names Linton. Soon after Isabella's departure, Hindley Earnshaw dies. Nelly ensures his funeral is respectable and cannot help wondering if her old master had "fair play" at the time of his death. Heathcliff is practically elated at Hindley's death, not least because as well as becoming master of Wuthering Heights, he now has Hareton completely under his control as he determines to "see if one tree won't grow as crooked as another, with the same wind to twist it!" (See *Wuthering Heights*, p. 206).

The next twelve years pass quietly enough at both houses. Cathy is a strong-willed child, but her willfulness is modified by her devoted love for her father and his gentle love for her. She is raised in complete ignorance of Wuthering Heights and Heathcliff. Upon Isabella's death, however, Edgar takes Linton to live at Thrushcross Grange. Heathcliff quickly comes to claim his son from Edgar.

Heathcliff's reasons for taking Linton to Wuthering Heights have far less to do with paternal devotion than they have to do with his plan to take vengeance on his old enemies. Linton is a sickly, "peevish" child, who does not seem destined to live long. Heathcliff tolerates his son because he is his son, though he considers Linton as having "nothing valuable" about him. He means, however, to make him go as "far as such poor stuff can go" (see *Wuthering Heights*, p. 240), using the boy to further his plans for revenge. Heathcliff plans for Linton and Cathy to "fall in love, and get married" (see *Wuthering Heights*, p. 235), thereby securing Thrushcross Grange for himself, he being Linton's heir should the boy die.

He encourages and contrives to strengthen the attachment between Linton and Cathy, convincing Cathy that Linton needs her because of his weak health and forcing Linton to play the part of an interested suitor. Though Linton likes Cathy well enough, he is far too preoccupied with his own sufferings and his fear of his father to truly care for anyone else. Cathy cares for her frail cousin, despite his ill temper and selfish whims, and it is easy enough for Heathcliff to entangle the willful girl in his plans.

Edgar and Nelly are against Cathy's romance with Linton as long as Cathy is required to go to Wuthering Heights to see him. Although Nelly fears Heathcliff, Edgar considers Cathy safe from Heathcliff's influence so long as she remains away from Wuthering Heights. Edgar is willing, therefore, to consider his nephew's suit provided that he comes to know the boy and that Linton visit Cathy at Thrushcross Grange. With his own health growing steadily worse, Edgar is concerned for Cathy and sees her match with her cousin as being a means of providing for her after his death.

As her father's health becomes very poor, Cathy remains with him, loath to leave his side even for Linton. Linton's health is simultaneously deteriorating, nearly as quickly as his uncle's. Heathcliff becomes desperate lest Linton die before marrying Cathy, threatening his "avaricious and unfeeling plans" (see *Wuthering Heights*, p. 280). He thereby, through Linton, arranges for the cousins to meet between Thrushcross Grange and Wuthering Heights, but Heathcliff tricks Cathy into entering Wuthering Heights.

Once Cathy is on the premises, Heathcliff keeps her there, forcing her to marry Linton, and attempts to keep her from her father's deathbed. Prevailing at last upon Linton, however, Cathy escapes in time to be with her father, who dies soon after her marriage. Heathcliff takes her to live at Wuthering Heights, where Linton dies a few weeks later.

Heathcliff has thus succeeded in gaining mastery over both Wuthering Heights and Thrushcross Grange. He also has power over the children of his enemies, making Cathy's life miserable and making a crass, uncouth farmhand out of Hareton. Heathcliff is yet, however, far from content. Ever miserable without Catherine, Heathcliff begins to see her everywhere. He becomes too distracted to eat, drink, or sleep. He is too distracted even to interfere with Hareton and Cathy's budding relationship. "I have to remind myself to breathe—almost to remind my heart to beat!" (see *Wuthering Heights*, p. 349) he tells Nelly, and he has reached the point where he has "lost the faculty of enjoying" the destruction of his enemies and "their representatives".

Heathcliff dies and is buried next to Catherine, leaving Wuthering Heights and Thrushcross Grange in peace. After Heathcliff's death, Hareton and Cathy plan their wedding for New Year's Day, a new beginning and the final victory of true love and justice over selfishness and revenge. "*They* are afraid of nothing", observes Mr. Lockwood. "Together they would brave Satan and all his legions" (see *Wuthering Heights*, p. 362).

Words Made Flesh: Summary of Critical Appraisals and Study Questions

The questions posed in this section are not intended for examination purposes but are designed to prompt appropriate trains of thought for the student to ponder as he reads the work. Questions intended for examination purposes are to be found in the "Study Questions on the Text" at the end of the study guide.

Joseph Pearce: Introduction to *Wuthering Heights*

Enough is known about the life of Emily Brontë, illumined by her letters, her poems, and her novel, to be able to know with some certainty that she was not the radical feminist, Marxist, or liberal that she is so often made out to be by her modern and postmodern critics.

Based upon the few facts known of her, that she was the quiet, home-loving daughter of a devoted parson, and the overall tone and meaning of her poetry, one can confidently conjecture that she was devoutly Christian in her beliefs and that her novel *Wuthering Heights* reflects this Christianity through and through. Though the story reflects the Hell that is formed through pride and unforgiveness, there is nonetheless the presence of Purgatory and Heaven, redemptive suffering and ultimate joy and happiness. For all its stark portrayal of evil, *Wuthering Heights* also gives the Christian answer to that evil. Emily Brontë is subtle in her depiction of Christian reality, yet for those with eyes to see, the evidence she gives not only of her own Christian convictions but of the overall Christianity of her work is more than apparent.

1. Although *Wuthering Heights* is commonly accepted as the passionate story of true love, with Heathcliff and Catherine being the heroes, Joseph Pearce seems to claim that such a reading is too simplistic. Would you agree that such a reading is too simplistic? Why or why not?

2. What is the foundation of Pearce's claim that the novel is a fundamentally Christian one? Is this validated within the text?

3. According to Pearce, what is the significance of Catherine's exchange with Heathcliff while on her deathbed?

Dedra McDonald Birzer: "Christian Love and the 'World Within' in *Wuthering Heights*"

Although often thought of as a passionate love story, *Wuthering Heights* is not so much a love story in the modern romantic sense. Rather, it is the story of familial love and the survival of that love despite the outside forces that threaten to rend it apart.

Raising numerous questions as to the nature of true love, Emily Brontë presents love as healing and permanent when it is self-sacrificing. The Earnshaws and the Lintons are seriously threatened by the presence of Heathcliff, and in the end, harmony and peace are recovered only through self-sacrifice and the death of Heathcliff, thus removing him from the picture. Upon his death and the marriage of Hareton and Cathy, the story has come full circle with peace having been restored as Cathy assumes the name of her mother, Catherine Earnshaw.

1. Birzer presents Heathcliff as the source of the strife within the novel. Do you agree? Do any of the other characters share responsibility for the strife?

2. Birzer claims that *Wuthering Heights* is about familial love and the destructive forces from outside that threaten to destroy it. Are all "outside" forces threatening to domestic peace and

happiness? If so, give your reasons for this belief; if not, discuss which outside forces might not be destructive.

3. Cathy and Hareton are able to marry only upon the death of Heathcliff. If it is the ghost of Catherine Linton that drives Heathcliff to his death, based upon your reading of the novel, do you think that this appearance of Catherine's ghost is for the sake of her daughter and family, or is it simply the fulfillment of her promise and Heathcliff's desire that she haunt him for all of his life, never leaving him? What difference, if any, does this make to Birzer's argument about self-sacrificing love and Heathcliff's relationship to the families?

Crystal Downing: "*Unheimliche* Heights: The (En)Gendering of Brontë Sources"

While many critics of Emily Brontë's *Wuthering Heights* have attempted to discover and prove the source of Emily Brontë's work, their conclusions have often been nothing more than mere conjectures, loosely founded (if founded at all) in the reality of Emily's life and the era in which she lived. Through examining the textual structure and elements within *Wuthering Heights*, in conjunction with the literature present within the Brontë home, Downing suggests three possible influences upon *Wuthering Heights*: Sir Walter Scott, Lord Byron, and Emily's mother, the strongest and most present being Emily's mother and the literature she left behind upon her death.

There are elements within Emily's story that bear uncanny resemblances to different stories her family is known to have enjoyed and explored in their youth. However, unlike an author who is consciously influenced by another in his own literary work, such that the work of one is but a tribute to the other, Emily Brontë's work was influenced and shaped by her own experience, most particularly by the presence of her distant, yet literarily familiar, mother.

1. In what way is Emily influenced by other authors, according to Downing? How is this evidenced in the text?

2. Downing calls the influence of Emily's mother on her daughter "umbilical". What does she mean by this, and in what ways, if at all, can this relationship be seen in the text?

3. What does Downing mean by "uncanny"? Where do you see the presence of the "uncanny" in *Wuthering Heights*?

Theresa M. Kenney: "Compassion and Condemnation in *Wuthering Heights*: Materialism, Christianity, and the Occult"

With Emily Brontë leaving the reader in complete ambiguity as to what she herself intended the moral of her book to be, the ultimate conclusion as to what the book really says about morality, Christianity, love, and passion is destined to be uncertain. Because it is impossible to judge the moral world in which the central characters move, it is impossible to determine a moral standard according to which they, and their actions, can be judged. Yet that seems to be the point in the end, that they cannot be judged by the reader just as they cannot be judged by each other within the book.

The two worlds most strongly portrayed within the novel are the Christian world and the pagan world, or the world of the occult, driven by passion and nature. The novel in the end does present a "clearly Christian" world, in which the standards of Christianity are reinforced. However, because the reader is left sympathizing with Heathcliff and Catherine, wishing them to be reunited (though not in Heaven but upon the "moors"), and more importantly, because the end is left hidden, *Wuthering Heights* must also most certainly be called an occult novel. The reader can judge what he thinks, yet like the characters within the novel, the reader is not left with any certainty that his judgment is the right one.

1. Kenney states at the beginning of her essay that the "authorial voice . . . is entirely absent". Yet Pearce, in his introduction

to the novel, insists repeatedly that Emily expresses her own Christian convictions throughout her work, notably in the voice of Nelly Dean. Based on your own reading of the text, would you agree that Emily Brontë is absent from her novel in expressing her own religious and moral convictions? Why or why not?

2. Is it possible to form an overall moral judgment of *Wuthering Heights* without judging the moral character of the individuals within it? In other words, can you judge the moral quality of the novel without answering the question of whether or not Heathcliff and Catherine acted morally or immorally? Explain.

3. Why does Kenney conclude that in the end, *Wuthering Heights* is an occult novel as much as it is a Christian novel? Based on your own reading of the text, do you agree with her?

Things to Think About While Reading the Book

The questions posed in this section are not intended for examination purposes but are designed to prompt appropriate trains of thought for the student to ponder as he reads the work. Questions intended for examination purposes are to be found in the "Study Questions on the Text" at the end of the study guide.

1. Dedra Birzer, in her essay "Christian Love and the 'World Within' in *Wuthering Heights*", quotes Lord David Cecil as saying that there is "a microcosm of the universal scheme as Emily Brontë conceived it" (see "Christian Love and the 'World Within' in *Wuthering Heights*," by Debra Birzer in *Wuthering Heights*, p. 370). in the contrasting, yet complementary, natures of Wuthering Heights and Thrushcross Grange. Cecil notes that while one house represents those born of the storm, who are wild and untamed, the other represents those born of the calm, who are tranquil and timid. Keep in mind throughout the novel what the cause of uneasiness, suffering, and unrest is. How is Thrushcross Grange affected by the unrest and misery of Wuthering Heights? Are there any parallels that could be drawn between the chaos and havoc of Wuthering Heights and the relative peace and tranquility of Thrushcross Grange? Consider particularly Nelly Dean's comment that "the mild and generous are only more justly selfish than the domineering" (see *Wuthering Heights*, p. 106). Can this be applied to the Earnshaw and Linton families, and if so, how?

2. In chapter 3 of volume 2, Isabella refuses to aid Hindley in his attempt to avenge himself upon Heathcliff, saying that "treachery and violence are spears pointed at both ends—they wound those who resort to them, worse than their enemies" (see *Wuthering Heights*, p. 195). Compare this with Ellen Dean's advice to Heathcliff at the beginning of the novel when he is musing on how he can revenge himself on Hindley: "It is for God to punish wicked people; we should learn to forgive" (see *Wuthering Heights*, p. 71). Pay close attention to the theme of forgiveness and vengeance within the novel, and to those characters who forgive and those who take revenge into their own hands.

3. The question of judgment and blame looms large within the novel, with no answer being given in the end as to the fate of, most particularly, Catherine and Heathcliff, nor of any other characters. In the meeting between Heathcliff and Catherine the evening before she dies, each accuses the other of various grievances. Be attentive to judgments and the consequences of misjudging or prejudging people within the book.

4. Most of the children who appear in the story suffer from negligence or abuse at the hands of their parents or other adults. Follow the direct consequences this has on the development of each character, particularly Heathcliff, Hareton, Hindley, and Linton.

5. *Wuthering Heights* centers around two families and the drama (or tragedy) of "love", that is, passion. Follow the theme of love throughout the novel: familial love, Christian love (charity), and the love between a man and a woman. What is true love? Who in the novel loves truly and purely?

6. Be attentive to the effects of suffering within the novel. How do various characters react to suffering? Who is hardened and

embittered? Do any characters benefit from their suffering? How does the suffering of Catherine and Heathcliff affect them? How do Edgar and Isabella respond to suffering?

Study Questions on the Text
of *Wuthering Heights*

Part One—Knowledge of the Text

1. Who is Mr. Lockwood?

2. "[Y]ou must e'en take it as a gift of God, though it's as dark almost as if it came from the devil." Whose words are these, and what is "it"?

3. What is the name of the puritanical old servant who speaks in a broad Yorkshire dialect?

4. How does Heathcliff get his name?

5. "Proud people breed sad sorrows for themselves". Whose characteristic wisdom is enshrined in these words?

6. Where does Catherine Earnshaw say she would be "extremely miserable"?

7. Who does Heathcliff marry?

8. "Nelly, I am Heathcliff". Who says these words?

9. What is the name of Heathcliff's son?

10. Who has room in his heart for only "two idols", his wife and himself?

11. Who adopted "a double character without exactly intending to deceive anyone"?

12. How does Heathcliff gain ownership of Wuthering Heights from Hindley?

13. Who "awakens or embodies" for Heathcliff a "thousand forms of past associations and ideas"?

14. When Lockwood returns to Wuthering Heights, what does he find Hareton and Cathy doing?

15. On what day is the marriage of Hareton and Cathy planned to take place?

Part Two—Essay Questions

1. Compare and contrast the Christianity of Nelly Dean and Joseph.

2. Examine the character of Catherine Earnshaw. How does her character develop throughout the novel? Compare and contrast her with her daughter, Cathy.

3. Compare and contrast the Earnshaw and Linton families.

4. Do the inhabitants of Thrushcross Grange contribute to the chaos and darkness of the novel or just suffer from it? Consider particularly Nelly Dean's comment that "the mild and generous are only more justly selfish than the domineering".

5. Examine the motif of haunting, demons, and diabolical natures (as Heathcliff is so often accused of having). What is the place of the demonic within the novel? What is the relationship between the demonic and the moral "hardness of heart" of the various characters?

6. The story of *Wuthering Heights* revolves around forgiveness and vengeance. What is the place of Christian charity within the novel? What are the effects of its absence? How is the vicious cycle of revenge ultimately ended?

7. Compare and contrast Heathcliff and Catherine Earnshaw's relationship with that of Hareton and Cathy Linton.

8. What does the novel say about familial love? Consider the various children in the story who are wronged and the effects this has upon the rest of their lives. In particular, examine Heathcliff's relationship with Hareton. What keeps him from loving the boy? How does Hareton respond? Does he love Heathcliff?

9. What does the novel say about judgment? Is anyone in the story innocent?

10. Is *Wuthering Heights* hopeful? If so, why; if not, why not?

———————————*Notes*———————————

Answer Key for
Wuthering Heights

Note to Teachers: This answer key can be removed before the study guide is given to the student.

STUDY QUESTIONS

Part One—Knowledge of the Text

1. Mr. Lockwood is Mr. Heathcliff's new tenant at Thrushcross Grange.
2. Mr. Earnshaw's words, speaking of the child Heathcliff
3. Joseph
4. He was given the name of a son of the Earnshaws who had died in childbirth.
5. Nelly Dean's
6. Heaven
7. Isabella Linton
8. Catherine Earnshaw
9. Linton
10. Hindley Earnshaw
11. Catherine Earnshaw
12. Gambling
13. Hareton
14. Reading
15. New Year's Day

Part Two—Essay Questions

1. *Compare and contrast the Christianity of Nelly Dean and Joseph.*

   The essay should address the puritanical aspects of Joseph's Christianity and the more "forgiving" Christianity of Nelly Dean. What are (if any) the extremes and deficiencies of each? How does each respond to the crises each family experiences? What does the response of each say about the Christianity of each?

2. *Examine the character of Catherine Earnshaw. How does her character develop throughout the novel? Compare and contrast her with her daughter, Cathy.*

   The essay should take into account not only the events in Catherine's life that were outside her control but also the numerous decisions she made that changed or confirmed aspects of her character.

   In comparing and contrasting Catherine with her daughter, it is critical that the role of free will is addressed, particularly in the capacity of each for love and forgiveness. Examine the strengths and weaknesses that are similar and different between the two, particularly in regard to how Catherine and Cathy react when presented with similar situations (do they react differently or similarly?). It will be necessary to address Cathy Linton's development in order to compare her with her mother.

3. *Compare and contrast the Earnshaw and Linton families.*

   This essay should examine the strengths and the weaknesses of each family, particularly in the way that the members relate to each other within their own families. How does each family member express love, forgiveness, or vengeance toward other family members as well as toward others outside the family? The Earnshaw family appears to feel the joys and tragedies of life more intensely than the Linton family; what contributes to this impression, and is it ultimately true? It is important to include the actual place where each family lives, as the home of each family symbolizes something about the character of that family.

4. *Do the inhabitants of Thrushcross Grange contribute to the chaos and darkness of the novel or just suffer from it? Consider particularly Nelly Dean's comment that "the mild and generous are only more justly selfish than the domineering".*

In this essay the actions of the Linton family need to be examined both in their motives as well as in their consequences. This essay should not focus so much on whether or not the Lintons are justified in acting as they do but rather on the way in which, if at all, they themselves contribute to the cycle of vengeance and unforgiveness through their actions. While the essay is not about justifying the Lintons, it is necessary to consider their motivations as well as their actions. Particularly consider the reception the family gives to Heathcliff at the beginning of the novel, the way the family members relate to each other throughout the novel, the way they respond to Catherine, and the way in which they respond to wrongs inflicted upon them by Heathcliff later on. Do Edgar and Isabella, and their parents, add to the conflict? Is there any other way in which they could have (or should have) acted?

5. *Examine the motif of haunting, demons, and diabolical natures (as Heathcliff is so often accused of having). What is the place of the demonic within the novel? What is the relationship between the demonic and the moral "hardness of heart" of the various characters?*

This essay should focus on the dimension of the unnatural within the novel and the way in which it is connected to personal sin. Catherine's ghost haunting Wuthering Heights and Heathcliff should be addressed, as should Heathcliff's "demonic" hold on the Earnshaw and Linton families as he seeks to destroy them. It is essential for this essay to keep in mind the deeply Christian dimension of the novel and its moral. This essay should examine the way in which Heathcliff, who is described as demonic, has placed himself outside the natural order of the world through his unnatural hardness of heart and pitiless determination to destroy his "enemies". What is it that makes a nature diabolical? Yet Heathcliff is not alone in his "hardness of heart": How do the sins of the various characters affect and build on each other? What is the connection, if any, between sin, the demonic, and acting against nature (i.e., being "unnatural")? The entire novel is heavily burdened by the cruelty and selfishness of its characters. To take revenge on one's enemies seems more natural than to leave that vengeance in the hands of another (God), yet what does the novel say about the true "naturalness" of taking one's revenge on one's enemies? How is it demonic, or in rebellion against the true nature of things?

6. *The story of* Wuthering Heights *revolves around forgiveness and vengeance. What is the place of Christian charity within the novel? What are the effects of its absence? How is the vicious cycle of revenge ultimately ended?*

Again, this essay must focus on the influence of Emily Brontë's Christianity on the novel. It is necessary to discuss not only the place of Christian charity but the nature of Christian charity as well. There are numerous examples throughout the novel of acts of charity, yet very few characters, if any, portray Christian charity, constantly and unselfishly. The story is mainly about the absence of true charity. Take into account particularly the character of Nelly Dean as she develops and matures throughout the story. What is true charity, and how is it revealed at the end of the book?

7. *Compare and contrast Heathcliff and Catherine Earnshaw's relationship with that of Hareton and Cathy Linton.*

   Many of the obstacles to Heathcliff and Catherine Earnshaw's relationship are present in the relationship of Hareton and Cathy Linton. Yet the difficulties presented to each are not entirely the same, despite Heathcliff's greatest efforts. In this essay examine the similarities and differences between Hindley and Heathcliff's relationship and Heathcliff and Hareton's relationship. Further examine the difference between the way in which Heathcliff and Catherine express their love for each other and the way in which Hareton and Cathy express their love. What are the differences and similarities between the way in which Catherine Earnshaw perceives Heathcliff and the way in which Cathy Linton perceives Hareton? Where does Catherine and Heathcliff's love lead them? And where does Cathy and Hareton's love lead them?

8. *What does the novel say about familial love? Consider the various children in the story who are wronged and the effects this has upon the rest of their lives. In particular, examine Heathcliff's relationship with Hareton. What keeps him from loving the boy? How does Hareton respond? Does he love Heathcliff?*

   The action of the story of *Wuthering Heights* is almost entirely driven by people unable to respond unselfishly to others. To what extent is this due to events during their childhood? Are they seeking revenge for wounds received in childhood? Ask this question, in particular, with regard to Heathcliff, Catherine, Hindley, and Linton. Each of these characters should be discussed in light of this consideration.

   In the case of Heathcliff and Hareton, examine Heathcliff's motivations and the manner in which he seeks to realize his revenge. Is Hareton's response what Heathcliff wanted? Is it different than he expected? Important to answering the last part of the question are Heathcliff's final days and the reaction of Hareton to him after he has died.

9. *What does the novel say about judgment? Is anyone in the story innocent?*

The essay should take into account the silence of the novel on the final end of Catherine and Heathcliff, as well as the numerous times in which judgment is mentioned throughout the novel. The question of whether there is a single person set up as judge within the story should also be addressed. What is the position of the reader? Is there a difference drawn within the novel between damning someone and judging one's actions as damnable?

10. *Is* Wuthering Heights *hopeful? If so, why; if not, why not?*

For this essay to be complete, there needs to be a reflection on hope. What is the nature of hope, specifically in the face of evil? That is, is resignation hopeful (as in the case of Hareton and Cathy while Heathcliff is still alive)? If the novel is hopeful, is it only at the end, or are there elements of hope throughout the story? Consider the relationship between Hareton and Cathy. Is it redemptive? Does the novel end on a happy note? Are the deep gloom and evil that permeate the novel up to the end adequately resolved?

Notes